~ May. '11

MW01048542

What We're Left With

(Special Dual Inscription Edition™)

Ben Murray

For Rosita,

~ Sense-ReAwakener, I write with you between my lines...

xxxxooo

For Rosita,

~ This book is for reading purposes only. Any attempt to defenestrate this book will be punishable to the full extent of the law.

&
BRINDLE
& GLASS

Library and Archives Canada Cataloguing in Publication
Murray, Ben, 1962–

What we're left with / Ben Murray.

Poems. ISBN 978-1-897142-29-5

I. Title.
PS8626.U774W43 2007   C811'.6   C2007-902550-1

The author gratefully acknowledges the editors of the following publications where
some of these poems first appeared: *Carousel, Contemporary Verse 2, The Dalhousie
Review, Descant, Event, Grain, Harpweaver, Queen's Quarterly, Quills, Whetstone, The Windsor
Review, Writers' Forum (U.K), and Zygote; the anthologies Oval Victory: The Best of Canadian
Poetry, Hortus Culturus (Poetry-On-The-Lake, Italy, 2003), 2001: A Space Anthology
(Cranberry Tree Press), and Witness: An Anthology of War Poetry (Serengeti Press, 2004).*

Cover photo: Tim Schumm
Author photo: Ron MacLellan

Brindle & Glass is pleased to thank the Canada Council for the Arts and the
Alberta Foundation for the Arts for their contributions to our publishing program.

Brindle & Glass is committed to protecting the environment and to the
responsible use of natural resources. This book is printed on 100% post-consumer
recycled and ancient-forest-friendly paper. For more information, please visit
www.oldgrowthfree.com.

Brindle & Glass Publishing
www.brindleandglass.com

1 2 3 4 · 5   10 09 08 07

PRINTED AND BOUND IN CANADA

The dead leave us staring with mouths full of love.
— Anne Michaels, "Memoriam"

You never know when you're making a memory.
— Rickie Lee Jones, *Youngblood*

Contents

I : WAR STORIES

Meanwhile the plum
blossoms trickling from above
through unresistant air
fell on my eyes and hair
as crimson as my blood
              —P.K. Page, "A Grave Illness"

what we're left with

it's the apples remembered most clearly.
ripe-red de-wormed apples still-lifeing the whirl
of aprons, open-shut fridges,
the suspense of *what's for dinner?* air

on this rooster-less farm, our dad
(six feet of sinew and workhorse and carrot-topped head
up with every dawn, all the rooster we needed),
a family harvested the years, the waspy drone
of wheat-weary tractors the only traffic
jamming the buzz of our ears

each year hundreds of round red births color-blinding
the green of orchards, awaiting windfalls
to graves of pie or the purgatory of deep freezers

years like this

then the world arrived
flat and white and sealed with no kiss,
my brother, eyes of ultra-blue to match
our biggest of skies, snatched
and flown to a place where the red runs
deeper than any *Macintosh*,
our ritual puke-up of *Delicious* and *Granny Smith*
a memory fading fast, bruised by the shriek
and crouch of orchardless lands
tilled and irrigated by sprays of fireworks

this brother dies there, limbs dancing in air
over the plant of metal bursting
ripe and desperate through teeming soil,
his blind and blistered feet
the pollinators of an angry energy

engineered to combat
battle fatigue, to bloody black earth

he returned to the farm, lighter now
his life a duffle bag army green
the clothy guts of him shrouded within

forever unopened, he lay uncoiled
unfoetally stretched across sheets
and quilts forever tucked in
untouched

mom left his door ajar, permanently,
each walk-by a shudder for eyes hoping
for some shift, some conjuring up
of lost flesh and blood

dawn cracked still, and chores
calloused the houring minutes,
but a world had knocked
on our sheltering doors and now
bits of it stunk the air
the seasons, stifling even the scent
of newly mown hay, and the wintering
warm of baking kitchens of 350 degrees

these times died, and now
in these post-farm years (a condo and
a convenience store weed the earth
where the farm once grew) I try to remember

my brother who died somewhere unpronounceable
for no relevant reason
try to remember the look of surprise

blown by unblue skies
that I've never seen, will never see

instead I always come back to the apples
apples bloating our summer bellies,
the way we'd bite into them hard
and thirsty, sleeving the drip
from our lips, tongue-teeth piercing
the hard vulnerable skins
until only the cores remained,
bruising fast in the revealed air

head-smashed-in buffalo jump, summer 2001

no bugs buzz the air here—
it's too hot,
our naked sandaled soles
fire-walking the baking earth

soon we are there, at the bluff,
at the drop where bison
by the thousands were herded
and forced to fly
for brief seconds,
before their great shaggy
heads broke old ground
in beds of bloodied dirt

we hold each other's waists hard,
for our dear lives feel dependent
on the other's reaching grasp—
there is no space here for lightness,
for the mock fall backwards

we're heavy as bison,
our spindly limbs
poor substitutes for wings,
our hot feet itching
to turn around and face
another future

my husband lies buried and i need to breathe

this park's afternoon mourns the death of
frisbee UFOs and lovers getting down
to grass's dirty level

John's dead and we all stand here,
stonehenged totems crying tears the perverse
perfect blue sky refuses to shed

the priest intones as a distant siren
swirls the air, signs of life
beyond the hearse's sigh

flowers and dirt are thrown up
and I wish he'd get up,
fight back, pitching clods back at us
a rose stem stuck in his teeth

did anyone else slip on black
underwear this morning, believing
the dead deserve to see?

various deaths

shorn of hair and shampoo
her bald head dries fast
in the tropical bathroom air

her waving hand parting
the steam-coated vanity,
she avoids the stranger's eyes
ghosting her mirror

Chase, Roamer, Smiley . . .
she thinks of the dogs she's had,
the kid-dogs, the single-life dogs,
Groucho, rugging the hallway
right now, married to her every move

thinks of her dogs' various deaths,
the pain, the wondering eyes,
the negative space they left behind

patting her face with
skin-creamed fingers, the white ooze
ghosting crease and line
she tries out a word,
watches her white lips mouth the name
of her late husband,
name and body and soul dead
for two years

tears rivering her cheeks, she anticipates
the taste of salt, tastes only the moisturizer
making-up her face

Groucho paws at the closed door
a muffled whimper;
she reaches over to turn the knob,
the cool bald brass slippery and white now
as she gets a grip

all the time in the world

I play games with the old

steal their canes, their clothes
their cataracts

imagine myself them
the body betraying me
one / Everest / step at a time

I hobble invisible
through a world bitten
by sound, by speed

at supermarkets   I count out
change, exact change, as if
there was all the time in the world

at buses I huddle   up-front
with other graybeards and bonnets
the back of the bus a foreign land

at home   in duplicate rooms
our old eyes window
life going on   outside

a bird perched on a branch
sings one of the old songs,
and I listen vainly
for the applause

photofinish

see, there we are, listening
to Sunday afternoon, our fingers
swords dueling over crosswords

there's me watering the palms
my naked baptizing arms a pale
shock against the jungling green

oh my, here's us in
bed, two fleshed whales
caught mid-breach
dripping waves

here's you dozing in church
head back mouth slack
never readier for revelation

oh   and there's you
with the Conlin girl, how sad
she looks, her hand lost
in yours, your eyes lost
in hers

and here's me
my face netted
by moist amen fingers

yes, and you in state,
in your only best, eyes
closed but I see them
blue-skied eyes open
darting about
through these walls

our house your eyes
I see the blue, your best

and forgive them,
this lone only time

toy gun

Gina points the gun like she wishes
it was real and I see the yellow
plastic bullet itching to be fired
by her curled fingers and even though
I know it's fake there's something
about a gun even a toy pointing
your way so I do my best Bruce
Lee and kick the gun out
of Gina's hand just as she fires
and as I fall back losing my
balance, about to hit the
floor I see the plastic yellow
bullet ricochet off the bald
head of our four-year old watching
tv who begins to cry as
Gina begins to laugh her hands
empty now and covering her mouth
the room full of crying, laughing
and my groaning as I reach back
and gingerly feel my bruised
tailbone, the emptied gun lying
a few feet away

maneuvers

tear and *tear* are spelled the same way
and this makes sense to me today
as I try not to cry
ripping his photos in half
before tossing them into the blue
recycling bag
amputated torsos and grins
keeping company now
with old news and tuna-unfriendly
tin cans ready for resurrection

mother always said it would end
this way, which is why I'm saving
one photo, him and I skiing in Banff
arm in arm, our blind-white grins
competing with the snow
ready to mogul off mountains
to blaze new trails.
this photo will remain awhile
framed above the fire, one toss away
from total immolation

she'll figure it out soon enough
his name untranslatable
into the language we speak
over the ordinary duties of dinner
and dishes,
she will flush me out
like the suburban Desert Fox she is
and I will surrender wearily, willingly
sudsy daughter's arms in the air
where she can see them

the white flags of my eyes
looking for mercy

the last yes

Syl is looking at me like a hitchcocking
bird, me the prey caught and cornered
in this room whose walls have heard
many things

a minute ago we lived in a different world;
this minute is a landscape bereft of familiars—
the bed, the dresser, the Matisse print bluing
the wall—my eyes seek their surety
but no soft landings now, everything
looks the other way

she asked and I told her,
the truth slipping out in a single syllable,
a wispy David of a word slain
by her Goliath gaze

I can't look at her, I look down
at my hands holding air,
the sheets below holding us aloft,
our tenting legs underneath

spisshhh!   I feel her spit strike my temple,
hot and wet I feel it trickle down
down over my cheek

as penance I let it sit there,
sitting here on this newly huge bed
the sound of domino doors slamming
the new soundtrack to my days

war issue

Dad always said there ought to be a graphic commemorative
stamp issue of the war wounded, the war dead. Red-leak
faces and bodies perforated by off-screen fire, the still of
their pain perfectly framed by tiny triangles, uniform and
white. Have people lick the gum-backs of a bloody stump of
a picture, receive love letters decorated with close-ups of
some poor sap's gut-spurt burst heart maybe then peace
would become the action, dad would say

my ears catch the grave tones of someone's boombox news,
as I walk which is why I think of dad and his bloody stamps,
and I remember vowing to forget all his windy veteran's
decrees how tedious they were to a boy marbling then
strutting then girling himself through eternal nows allergic to
clockwork whiskeyclouds vulturing our no-name home and
mom and me

a mosquito copters down onto the pad of my arm-flesh

as it proceeds to suck up my Type A
I fight the desire to crush it, like the enemy

occupation

my baby's been planted in a rock garden
silent as a plant my baby lies under brick
at first he cried *mama* and cried
but now he's stopped and I know
all these men in shades of green scurrying around
they must have watered my baby they must
be experts on growing things because
you always hear about people with green thumbs
well these men they're all green like big tall
blades of grass except they can move, they
can move around their pale faces all angled
skyward into the sun

I hope the sun lets my baby look
at its magic yellow face and grow quick
and strong like a weed like all these
green men

when I asked one of them if he had seen
my baby he pointed one smoking cigarette
finger up to the sky and then crossed his chest
like he was praying for rain

home fronts

sitting here, eyes to ceiling skies
we imagine the china music of
other wars, teacups rattling
in their trays, the Crosley Bullet
reassuring, melodious, as it describes
all the hues of red

now we sit powerless
before a dead internet,
insubordinate computers ignoring
our curses, cursors flipping the bird
at commands across the land

a snatch of music wafts our way,
and I think of that old ad: *Is It Live,
Or Is It Memorex?* and I fight back tears
knowing it can be neither, just some trick
of wind and mortar

the dog, long past due his walk,
sits and stares at us with sad and
uncomprehending eyes, a spreading
stain of piss darkening his blankie,
its brief gift of warmth a lie

the ride

the taxi driver was telling me
how the world was gonna end,
but I could only count the meter
swallowing the blocks, the thick
security of my wallet an illusion
losing ground, fast

he went on and on, like he was
paid by the word
and I tried to focus
on whiz-by neighborhoods
on the life picturing car-door windows

at a red light his voice finally stops
with the car
and the loud quiet tempts me
to open the door and flee,
saving some bucks
and my ears

but of course I just sit there,
the car and his drone all revved up
and ready to go with the green,
my head back on the seat
looking up at the vinyl roof, stained
by miles of words with nowhere to go

colville's man

you want to remember that Colville
the gun on the table foregrounding
the shirtless man, sleek back framed
by an ocean-view window, a wave
caught mid-churn

was it even a hotel room?
that's how you remember it,
something transitory in the clean
quiet of metal and skin—
a place to live with decisions made
however briefly

the ocean here is even more painterly

Colville's man, cropped at the neck
looked so relaxed, so at ease, the gun
a prop, pointing stage left

you want to remember that Colville
so you can relax cool and collected
like that shirtless man,
past and future subordinate
to the waves shoring this hotel room,
foreground guns simply foreground

breaking the surface

birds swim in angel pee
she says, and I laugh
realizing I will never look
at my old sky again
will always see hers
tinkling clouds and stars

I follow her down paths
we've grown up forging,
the Mackenzies and Moodies
of this small world
our ravine

we reach the lake
scramble up our favourite
rise, where scores of
Olympic diving records
have been broken
in our minds

we talk awhile
certain names frowning her lips
and I wish them buried
under the baked sandy earth
we sit upon

my sister goes first
and as she jumps I imagine her
shedding the skins
of all those boyfriends weighing
her still-teen body down
their leather-and-cologne-clad forms

caught wingless, suspended
over this grotto
the look of comic-book
surprise as they look down
realize they are falling
splash towards the water

their faces waves
watching impotently
as my sister
only my sister
breaks the surface,
her body dripping smiles

the licorice man

my son believed in the Licorice Man
because I told him about how
the Licorice Man changed color
from black to red to black again
whipping his twisty long body
into a fine frenzied twirl the faster
and faster he spun the less
of one color and the more of the other
you'd see, bits of red or black
flying off and sticking to walls
and floors to be collected later
by the candymen and sold
to little boys and girls chewing
the red or black wands and wondering
how anything paid for with pennies
could taste so fine

now as I make the long drive
to where my grown son lives
his life skyless, surrounded
by wall-to-wall other guys
in for five to ten or twenty to Life
I look at the whiz-by green
windowing my car, wish I could
bottle the green for him to see
to inhale when he needs to smell things
more than stale indoor air
the scent of womenless men
some of whom may miss the grass
as they trade favors, bum smokes
and count the hours
under the ghosting fluorescent stare
of other sad men, who work there

I wait, as the guard
rifles through my offering,
try to blot out the sight
of the guard's callous hands
fingering the red and black swirls
which the Licorice Man
had twisted and spun
especially for my son
only, my son

deep pockets

i've spent
the last
of my
coins

tonight
i'll dig
for
moons

II) 20,000 BREATHS

I am a panther shut up and bellowing in
cement walls, and I am angry at blue
evenings without ventilation
                    — Charles Bukowski, "A Report
          upon the Consumption of Myself"

senseless

how bright the light
of mornings
moving across floors and eyes
in denial of the vertical

this and the honky *swish*
of clockwork cars
drunk on gas
and traffic jam
disarms the real-world
buzz of the alarm

a PJ-clad, bedheaded
body stands by the window
the curtains part
and he's blinded
by sun-ripe chrome
and concrete

should they look
passersby would see
a pane-glass man
hands covering his eyes

one sense down
four more to go

suburban snapshots

a man sees a pile of raked leaves—
stops, looks both ways,
then takes a running jump into the huge pile

a frothing dog chases a trespassing cat
over its fence, into the cat's yard
where another cat and dog sleep entwined, on a hammock

somebody's grocery-toting mom drops a ketchup bottle
smash! onto the driveway; watches mesmerized
as the red ooze slowly drowns a daddy-longlegs

a team of softballers take turns hugging
their sobbing coach, who's just had
his testicles removed

two teens attempt to break the record
set by Ted and Jen last weekend—
with three witnesses and a case of cola,
they begin their marathon fuck

a Dickie Dee ice-cream bike pulls over
quiet, no bells; its driver opens the freezer,
feels around and pulls out a frosty DQ shake

a boy is beaned by a basketball—as he falls back onto
the leaf-strewn lawn he remembers the huge pile of leaves
he raked earlier, how it could have cushioned his fall

garage sale

the garage has ruptured,
its guts spilling into the alley

cars snake by slowly
they can't not look
some of the braver even
park, ask questions

we sit on lawnless lawn chairs
lord and lady of this patch of pavement,
the spoils of our kingdom
yours, for a price

next weekend we will decide
the boy is old enough
to handle our divorce,
but for now

we are all business,
married to the small profits
to be made discounting the past,
the satisfied smiles of strangers

a kind of connection,
a kind of intimacy

like life .

It's evening and you sit on the deck
eating a late dinner, a small radio
at your side for ambience

the news sounds old so you thumb
the dial until a tune catches
your fancy, somebody's blues

or is it soul? you can't tell anymore,
everything's everything these days,
you want pure, buy bottled water

for four quarters guzzle
the piss of glaciers

your hands shaking like leaves
remembering the dream when nothing
came out of your faucet

but the dirty-brown blood
and guts of trees, the porcelain air
smelling like life

new growth

Signs of life: rubber ficus tree
sprouts new smooth-pink leaf
shaft, coiled, ready-to-spring
blood-green slice of jungle into

here, this parch-white jack-
in-the-box, where air comes
conditioned, and rain sleeps
in metal beds

where a man glances, glacially
at his advancing fingernails,
realizing   they must
be cut

dead endings

the shoulders of highways
carry the burden of crashed cars, of
crashing relationships white-lining
escape routes,
exhausted air breathing heavy
not breathing at all
under Trans-Canada skies

you whiz by roadwreck
the cherry siren swirl,
refuse to crane your neck
instead squeeze your partner's
hand   *see, we're alive*

it's all in the rear-view now
only exists if you choose
to look up and catch the shimmer
of sun-caught chrome on pavement,
the smoke signaling nothing
the people in that car deader
than you are

strewn in token tabloid poses
the taste of decaf
of light cigarettes lying
wasted, untasted behind the shock
of their finish-line mouths

tonight you will come with a force
forgotten since teen years,
the slick surprise milking the flat flora
of your pillowcase

your partner highways away
in your shower, eyes stinging
a little blinded
by the shampoo in her eyes

20,000 breaths

On average, we humans take roughly 20,000 breaths a day.
— *Alive Magazine*

night wakes
in a daze
to sog-white mornings
of caffeinated mouths
mating *Cheerios*
O to empty *O*

news oozes snap-crackle gloom
like it was still dark,
day-glow ghost stories
with no ghosts, no story

pink shower-flesh
pisses the last
of last night
down dipsomanic drains

pores, open now
watch limbs drape themselves
in cling-free fabric
as disasters give way
to the weather, a triumph
of the mild

paving, roadster eyes
straddle 4-wheels
as bumpering metal thrusts
and parries,
thrusts and parries

just before forgetting,
he decides tomorrow is the day
he'll count each and every one
of his 20,000 breaths

33

perspectives

ants come to me, on hands
on knees, asking for direction

birds fly over me, thinking
Avoid Trees That Walk

my cat sniff-licks me
remembering Egypt

and mirrors laugh
when i'm not looking

cat standard time

for Olin, Braque, and Emily

cats are soft clocks watching
time play with windows
and the warmth of day-seen stars

our hands move by the minute
by the hour, sculpting tension's
release out of the furred smooth

prowling 'round carpet forests
their Point B crouches, invisible
to our Point A

looking into their eyes, we see
savannah tails twitch and conduct
a restless, wild music,   time

the space you fill between meals

amnesties

some kid's knees scratch red-letter pain onto pavement,
a skateboard enjoys a few minutes' freedom
nestled in grass, just wood, a board again

across the street a panting tongue watches, too bored
to bark, daydreams of collared leather snipped in two

off-track Indy cars whiz by, trapped, impatient,
speeding towards flags and finish lines, towards the
roar of crowds

a wind picks up, whips dozens of shiny flyers
from the hands of their deliverer,
2 For 1 Family Dining papering driveways
and trees

inside homes, televisions watch their owners
plot their prime-time escapes

some kid screams in pain just a few seconds
too long   tomorrow
he will ask for a new skateboard

at home at a foreign film

outsize telephones, black and endangered, ring
across the blocks
exchanging close-ups, itching
to use the perfect
pickup line

technobeats bass the beat
of hearts, tugged
from one Ikea showroom
to another

lovers lift tired flesh
off flesh, check their skins
for war-wounds red-wet, and visible
ignoring bedpost notches
nailed to the wall

imploding tears tick
like time bombs in reverse
the mute hide-and-seek whimper
which follows big bangs

a man screams subtitles
out his window,
the world, the woman
walks on, oblivious
the high-angle amber glow of a cigarette
signaling life lived
between stop and go

a cat suddenly leaps, furs
your air, begins its kneady
spiral lap-dance
each little belly-claw
every tuna-breath exhale
a reminder to rewind

donor

the wine must be his type,
it feels so good as it slicks
reddens his insides

his eyes suddenly see
like one of those throat-cams
see the liquid as it streams
past tissue and vessel
filling hollows

somewhere somebody is filling
plastic with their liquid blush,
the promise of cookies
and a hero's conscience
scant *cc*'s away

he pours another, peers
into the red pool glass

sees nothing but the wine

a mosquito lands there
begins to drown,
wet wings stilled
by this false heaven

he tilts back the glass,
drinking it all in

scene of the crime

love's chalk line lies on the floor—
last night's underwear giving up the ghost
as sunlit blinds look the other way

the room is a Weegee without the flash—
an open door, a disheveled bed, and a man
glazing the walls with witnessed eyes

he can still smell her in the room—
the sheet he clutches smells like her
her second skin, losers weepers

the bed is a wound his mind must scar—
home videos are rewinding
but he will not hit PLAY

when he finally gets up he'll treat himself—
flipping pancakes to the news
he'll pick and choose his headlines

phonely

you're there, perched
on my shoulder, talking
in my ear, and i whisper
into the breath-black
plastic ear, i mutter a muffled
curse to A. Graham Bell, that Great
Tease, enticing one sense
leaving the other four
on staticized hold

your voice a painting in Braille
for a seeing man, behind glass

i would hang up, listen
to your echo leap its last
from the high of wires
me free of deprived senses
heart re-opened, for play

instead, you say
"what was that?"

"oh, nothing," i respond
my lips puckered kiss-like
over the "oh"

the single death

naked toes carefully navigate
carpeting cats littering him
with plush meows

forgotten greenery quietly shrieks
for water, browning finger-fronds
extended, pleading

last month's news strikes tragic
poses, piled and spilling
onto kitchen linoleum

scanning microwaved wallkill
he counts stains, each as piecemeal
as pot-shy, as the rest

he slips in two slices of *Wonder-*

seconds later the premature pop
of a single white
toast
spongy and spotless,
christens the token afternoon

day for night

this is how it always starts—

the clock, having nightmared it was
a clock, buzzes itself awake
a silencing palm sending it back
to the relentless hell
of tick, of tock

in the shower you watch
your flakes of night-skin washed
off your body, sucked
into the thirsty vortex slurping your toes

the sun blooms outside your kitchen window
but you flick on fluorescence anyway
because it's there, the morgue-white
light giving your microwaved meal
an extra intensity a glow sorely missed
by taste-lax buds
wilting in the dark

across placemat headlines you glance
at your partner, newly fresh and reborn
like you and the world outside,
the dewy twitch of night-dreams
scorched and burned in the pale of day

at the door, caffeinated mouths mate
smack like pros with eyes closed
the flesh of night-lips
just another aftertaste

in the elevator, briefcased and vertical
the glare of the overhead bulb
obscures your watch's face for a sweet minute

time was

> The world is so complicated, tangled, and overloaded
> that to see into it with any clarity you must
> prune and prune
> > —Italo Calvino, *If on a winter's night a traveler*

The city was a town was
a village was a house was
a frame was a tree was
a forest was that

me as a child happy
with the one toy
the simplest toy a ball
or an empty box my own
pudgy fingers and lips
touching and tasting the cribbed
world the whole world
in my grasp, was that

a gunshot just now?
a car backfiring?
or was that someone's
surround-sounding movie
way too loud, was that
maybe my own television
not loud enough? was that

really my wife who
just walked out the door
with the kids saying
it's over, it's over?

tomorrow I will rub tired
sleepless eyes with pudgy fingers
focusing ahead
on the one toy

III) THE WHOLE EARTH AN INN FOR THE NIGHT

All night the truth happens.
— Michael Ondaatje, "Country Night"

How can we sleep while our beds are burning?
— Midnight Oil, "Beds Are Burning"

brand new world

There's a mickey in the tasting of disaster
— Sly Stone, "In Time"

exhausted cars will continue wheezing by windows
as Verne and Wells swap flyleaf dust
on the shelves of libraries reaching, Borges-like
into skies higher, higher, planing towers
lighthousing the traffic of air with the blink
of neon, emission-grays climaxing days
of hover and sigh seen
but not heard from streets, straight-angle
streets whose only green captures billboard eyes
squinting at trees, flat-photo trees which brailling
men and women could never sliver or sap as they
run parched hands and fingers over this and that
all this, all that the same genetically modified
plastic pavement seducing the souls of Nikes
running, racing towards finished lines
the roar of crowds, the tickering tape which fails
to burst apart as your body inches forward
fails to burst, apart, because
it's unbreakable tape, designed not to break
under pressure

and the last birds will sing
of sitcoms 'til sundown
of the black-eye blood of tabloids, inc.
of guns for teacher and apples for Monsanto
of the peopling rush hour crush of urban subs
scoping out our mundane terrain

sing, of last tigers as they explore the four corners
of their brand new world

foundations left

down the street an old house
expodes, the invisible silver
of its lining raining down
on audiences
of hard and yellow hats

motes of memory
catch the sun's rays
for a first time,
the shock of freedom
blasting apart the cornered
comforts of a history

a bird arrives, surveys
the shift, the emptied air,
the shadow of its wings carving
releasing brief lives as it swoosh-
glides over rubbled brick
and mortar

tweet once, tweet twice
the signal given, that this
new nowhere is no place
to perch

the skycrack hats disassemble,
a bird flies off, after new angles,
and a demolished house continues
to explode

the man who lost the news

he rides his loud bike in the PM shower
(the bike squeaks and clangs but never bullies air
like cars, cars that could crush him
and his bike, creating instant pavement
juice trickling from his brain
into worming curbside drains)

rides past glow-box windows
where life flickers muted behind curtains
between commercials,
hears choke-chain dogs barking
their drooly love of these prime-times

rides all the way to the ocean,
skid-thirsty tires spitting up wet
well-sandaled sand, bike chain choking
on this fast-food snack
of the slow death of dry

counts twenty steps to the frothy lick
of water's edge, stands there awhile
listening, watching, in vain
for some kind of commentary

simply grass

I lie flat
stomach to the stars
arms and legs outstretched,
a grassland Gulliver
made captive by earth's
deep thrum, the hum of ants
the snore of gophers

it is night, and this high grass
hammocking my form
could be any color,
green a dream
in all this deep dark

in the morning, light
will gift this world
and the names of things
will dawn:
Galium boreale,
Thomomys talpoides

but tonight, nothing
is named, nothing owned
my flesh simply grass
rooted in the loamy black
waiting for nothing

ascendant

up here the sun tips my fingers, you are that close

the sun the moon the stars inches away from the grasp
of your emptying hands, the filling of heart and soul
a gradual slow rush paid for with lost-track switch-
backs bisecting the rooty dust kicked up by
blister-packed heels, feet like Cambrian fossil rock forced
to move again against the centuries, the pain of awakened
joint and bone and skin more and more forgotten with each
step made closer to the summit the peak the air thinning
thinning as the forever greens of trees shrink to shrubbery
the occasional gentian coloring slate-slab stone the rockbound
squeal of pikas a reminder to forget other sounds
like the sound of your car door as it slams shut
in the Gore-Texed parking-lot lawns kilometers below

but you don't think of that now, you've forgotten it again
the pika whistling warnings as you step heavily through
its backyard scree the sky expanding with each step
you tilt your head back and guzzle glacial water drinking
it all in the sky the air the water the knowledge
that another few feet and you're there on top of this mountain
this great glorious rupture of rock
your hands gripping a cairn you're holding on
for this dear life that surrounds you now every direction
a view never seen before, other peaks valleys glaciers rivers
spread before you growing into your eyes your swallowing
brain dosing over and under the sun
tipping your fingers,
that close

a kind of sleep

    Science magazine says over a quarter species
    gone in the next twenty-five

    and i'm counting the gasolining miles
    cars live and breathe, exhausted roadside
    trees sick and tired of playing punch buggy

    fossil fish, ferns, trilobites:
    a silent slate chorus occupying
    my apartment's many layers
    greets me upon my return

    i ignore them, heading straight
    for the bedroom; clothes shed
    in a molting pile bedside, i lose
    myself in blankets and pillows
    which slowly warm me, by degrees

    my naked fetal form soon sweating
    through a kind of sleep

journey's end

some few years from now
the last wild grizzly
will scoop up its pawed and clawed
reflection from some wild river,
one last time before

shedding most of its fur
shrinking its bulk
reshaping its brain
and slipping on pants
and a shirt

it will make its way to the
strange roar of the city,
where it will find work
and buy things wrapped
in dead trees

these it will load into its
pine-scented motor-box, before
roaring over forests
of white-line grey

he'll pull up to his den
smelling of pine-scented
air and wood, that
closets and buffers

later he'll switch off the light,
powered by neither sun nor moon
and try to sleep, amongst electric-white
sheets and sky-blue pillows

restless, he'll arise,
scoop up metallic water
to his shrunken snout

and catch its reflected glimpse
in glass, realizing now
just how he's come up
in this living, breathing world

sure signs

yesterday we plugged Nik into an Extinction learner-module
just to quiet him down for awhile

our mistake

midnight we're woken to his crescendo cries
his six-year old arms fighting off the resurrection
of grizzlies, cougars and great apes, a take-a-number
line-up of extinct animals spooring and pawing the fertile
ground of Nik's nightmare mind

it's just us, we soothed, there's no such thing as...
the three of us one big hug for awhile,
comfort regained in an octopus of arms

after Nik slipped back into sleep
we made slow love, our eyes locked together
in what could only be the look of love,
and for a blessed few released seconds I'm convinced
she's real, that Nik's real, that
my shot sperm has a purpose still,
the recorded wind rattling the panes
a sure sign of life

freefall

. . . and every country below is an I land
— F R. Scott, "Trans Canada"

must others too fight the desire
to elbow-smash past plane panes
and be sucked whole out of
sterile dead air into the head-
quaking rush of currented
breathing air that instantly fills
each starving pore, your goggle-eyes
and balloon-brain bursting
with the wonder, the glory
of the shapes and contours
and textures of just one point
on a planet that speaks
to no one in particular
except this one flightless bird
that soars and sinks, like a man
for whom meaning has finally
been found on the shores of
somewhere in particular

to fall to rise

the gate opens, and he begins
his grateful early morning fall in-
to the dawning scrimmagings
of this park

his favorite bench sits
still daubed in dew
his nestling ass a mop
for sun-shy wet
frying in the hours

surround-sound birds begin
singing his praises
and he rewards them
with bread and seed-song
notes on the fly
crumbling the air

the birds disperse
he sits back, watches
risen trees
chlorophyll the air
their green architecture
a true balm

for a man who's fallen
between too many cracks
in the façade
his spirit renewed each a.m.
with the iron squeak
of the gates, opening
welcoming him back in-
to the world

communion on hornby

hijacked bald eagles nestle
the Canadian coast, wide-screen wings
spread over phosphate-friendly tides
washing cleaner clean grains of sand

their high-angle cries echo my eyes
as I lie back making snow angels
in the sand; I soar and dive, and talon
slippery fish with them

the whitecaps of their regal staring
heads harbor all the colors of an earth;
blinded by the 6pm sun, by these birds'
star-sized eyes

I dig myself deeper into cool sand,
footprints and the distant swish
of getaway cars gradually receding
with the time

the lake had swallowed fire

and as I looked up from the wet
waterlogged sun to the dry disc
blinding the sky

I thought of those men, alien
in their slo-mo suits, walking
ponderously on the moon

and how easy it would be
to dive headlong into the sun
my sleek-naked form rippling
radiant water, exploring
pores wide open breathing in
the illusion that whatever we do
is necessary

living in the dead of winter

in these globally warmed days, spring
sprouts its lovely head, living
in the dead of winter

how long until hibernating bears
shake November from their sleep-under fur
and start snouting around for off-season
bargains, the juice of surprised berries
bloodying the melt of snow

kids' snowpants will no longer chafe
breath-defying thirty below,
polyester cocoons mothballed and closeted,
a clear case of death by hanging

migrating birds and people will stop
migrating, their travel agents sitting idle,
bored behind postered windows,
winterless southern climes cooler now
than winter

beery bellies and sunblock bikinis
burn baby, burn
under ozone suns,
the death of winter dangling lynch-'em style
from some driver's jingle-jangle
car-key fingers

returning the hug

in times of trees i listen
to bark breathe
against my back

eyes closed i see leaves
in relief fanning
a sweating sky

my shoes and socks molted
in a forgotten pile, pale
feet dig cool in shady
grass, exfoliating blades
whose green blood dyes
the dying skin

the tree has postponed
my melting—
i arise and embrace
cliché, arms hug-holding
on this dear life

and i am also
the passerby, embarrassed
at this public display,
anywhere-but-there eyes
trying to find a way
through the heated world

the forest and the fire

smoke pyres the eyes,
the absence of birds
cataracts in the sky

the air is a fireplaced
living room with no chimney
no flue, every breath
a sigh

your steps kick up the traces
of ashen animals,
motes of memory leaping
their last

last night here
a tossed cigarette
returned to the trees,
its amber eye
glimpsing the future

boreal song

mum birds play
who will sing first?
the quiet here the quiet
of clear-cut answers
and ravines

the sun is now
the whole story,
mysteries of mulch
and canopy timbered
into afterthought

the pines that remain
almost as perfect
as the scent and shape
of rear-view dangle

wounds this open
close only in dreams
held like worlds of
dew in the beaks
of birds who once
would sing

foolish notes sung
octaves above
the earth,
and falling, scattering
like seeds

the best time

A gardener's profile spades the waning light
knees digging into fresh soil
she turns over old leaves an inch at a time

this is the best time, she thinks
the noises of the day walled up,
muffled, heads beginning their nightly nod

as the darkening earth gifts her
with its revealed musk
her under-nails teeming with black life

she forgets what she's been planting—
enough that the seeds fill her palms
with their light

temptation

i spare the browning parchment leaf
from a shoe's temptation,
crouch down and pick up
the once-green brown by its stem
giving it a last-time twirl
in the falling air

it is sunday and there is an almost
quiet on this block baring its trees
for grateful audiences
of waxwings and sunday walkers
digesting the noon

no one is there to notice
as i bring the leaf to an ear
holding it there cupped, shell-style,
hearing a forest's wind
rustle lobe and drum

and soon i feel my hand
close in on the leaf
crushing it into the finest powder

to touch lakes

i've tried to touch lakes
still-life lakes immune
to paint-by-number tourists
and the shuttering clicks
of their single eyes

touch them with bashful
thirsty hands, eager
for the baptism of loons

but each time a finger
pokes the surface
wrinkling the wet smooth

i think of swimming-pooled
flesh, of acid rain

and my baited fingers return
glistening, slick, untouched

the whole earth an inn for the night

distance is a lie

astronauts pluck this planet
from skyless skies, their eyes
never wider as they marvel
at the ease with which
they can tuck in this planet,
ice caps poking lazily out
from under a blanketing moon

but tonight, in your science fiction
suit of armor, you're umbilicaled
to the hull, sparking space
and a tiny tear with solder.
lots were drawn
and you won the draw
so here you are, the lucky one

your heart swells
with the remembered smells
of your mother's sweet milk,
the jungling fur of nappy cats
of lovers' laps,
the mold-fresh scent of forests
meters/minutes away from the dawn
jaws of chainsaws buzzing
their way 'til dark

and as you glide back
into this ship's heart
faceplate steamy with tears,
you dare not look back
over your shoulder,
the whole earth an inn for the night

IV) MEMORY DEAREST

In my dark room the years
Lie in solution,
Develop film by film.
Slow at first and dim
Their shadows bite
On the fine white pulp of paper.
— Ann Wilkinson, "Lens"

smelling lilacs

over thirty years to learn to smell
    the lilacs . . .

what was smelled in baby, in boydays?
In pre-man and early-man days?
    shit, milk, *Downy*
chlorinated pee, clove-fed Christmases
blood of skateboard-skinned knees
piny mountain air, old-comic must
    nougat, licorice, *Breck*
math-examined sweat, sawdusty guinea pigs
womaning girls in their clean teen-skins
    toast, socks, *Testor's*
spitty sax reeds, unSuite basments
vaginized fingers, the stiff rigid air
of first funerals, of weddings

this nose no slacker, so why now, only
now with the lilacs?

this intoxicant the resurrection
of smelled-it-all, in-your-face
olfactories, nostrils performing grateful
flaredances for the rest of you

reborn now every spring with the lilacs
middle age will spread its sweatering arms
in hugs of full body, nose a bit off
to the side, smelling
what sweetly demands
to be smelled

memory dearest

craving certain summers
whose kite-crazy barbecued
air could be bottled
and sold, 10-cent stand-style
as

That Vintage Season—
pull the cork, and
divine a time, when
the two-wheel clickity-
clack of spoken
clothespinned playing cards
was the coolest

the most quenching
sound around

some Thing

the rink reminds him of those Thing movies,
the monster born of blocks of ice thawing
into another world, our world, where whiteout
horizon lines bisect the eye, 360

there is no monster here in this outdoor rink,
though the cacophony of kids' shrieks could fool
a blind Sherlock; how similar the cries of glee
of anger, of fear

his cousin once mocked him by telling friends
he couldn't skate "because he was scared a monster
would come up from beneath the ice and eat him"

it got a good laugh; and now

as he laces up old skates whose newly polished
blades gleam like the ice they'll soon slice,
he almost wishes some Thing would materialize,
its outstretched arms coming towards him
like a hug from another world

run, run, rabbit

those were mall-free days, when bored boys
flicked their tongue-tales out of doors,
washing down their summery freedom
with bottled pop and a Freezie,
teenage iguanas on sugar highs

the sneaker-squished flat grass of Corbett Park
beckoned, not a tree in sight, we the resurrection
of trees felled by the wild roar of urban chainsaws

sprawling languid under a pre-cancerous sun,
limbs exhausted with the to-do of nothing,
we hurry up and wait, to become men

just before that signal event,
a jackrabbit bounds across our field
of view, and we give chase
6 legs after 4

outsize ears swept back by its
created wind, it runs, runs, spooked
the wild of its fur a dirty-brown blur
before our bulleting eyes

before our eyes, rabbit, cornered
leaps the fence, its pogo-stick paws
landing   *plofff*
silent as sight, onto grassless whiteline
black, meant for no mammal

the car that smashed into our prize
sent it leaping one last time
was a Volkswagen

a couple of us enjoyed rabbit stew
that night

another, after ten more years
of indifferent luck
threw out his rabbit's foot
and became a vegetarian

navigator

the promise of water lies liquid
under the rinked lake,
my big boots gum-boats
floating feet over ice

mom's voice calls out
from another world,
a shoreline shout
warning over breath-seen air

I don't turn around,
I keep walking,
each new step
hope for the next

at the lake's center
I lie down, stomach on ice,
four feet of toque, down
and wet jean docking the big white

head to the side, a woolen ear
listens to the ice,
listens to the promise of water
raging beneath

the rest of me waits
for the received cry,
the revealed thaw,
the ice aging
by the minute

wish

you make the past
a wish of a child
whispering air
like loose down

May soon forgets
April
and nobody wants
a 24-hour moon

yet here we will always
be, mid-kiss

arms steepling our heads
4 hands made 2

arms in the air
with the answer

the blue blouse

so i finish with the dishes
start with the laundry
. . . folding, sniffing, sorting . . .
and as i hold up your
blue blouse, reborn and
smelling of the sun
you come up behind me
arms encircling my waist
hard, like you're trying to
squeeze me breathless
and you start to giggle
like the high school sweetheart
i never had, and i laugh too
falling back against you
both of us falling back
onto the tumble of sheets
and shirts, your blue blouse
flung in the air briefly
before landing
on our sprawled bodies
like the lightest of blankets

a nephew's painting on the wall
for Mooshkabob

is there a blue beyond these walls
as blue?

a good-day sky is shy a tone or two this
ultra-marine; perhaps the deep Nemo-seas
of Verne or Pixar come close

close to a nephew's blue
on bachelor walls, a
twelve-inch landscape in oil of five pines
standing sentry to an exploding sun,
green and yellow this blue's second thought

the painting is ten years old now,
its painter grown, no longer the boy
cornered in his dad's studio playing
with brushes, brushing against dad's
smeary easel legs

he's navigated the Nintendo years,
the first kisses, the clicks of ignition
and recognition, the laws and love as set
by parents whose features morph his own now
as he begins to shave and trim, time

does he miss the blue?
remember it even?

a couple years ago he saw the painting
hanging there beneath picture windows;
he barely glanced at it
as if embarrassed at the sight of some

first crush, the blush of an earlier you
un-summoned, awkward

i will look at it for him, waiting
for that moment when the pines
outgrow the sky

by the graveside of a famous painter
did she try her luck
for Margrit

She threads her way
carefully, feet balanced
on tightrope trails that
snake past rocks of perfect
rectangle, of beveled arch

she has a destination
that's clear; perhaps one
of these quiet monuments
has her name on it, or
maybe she's just a visitor
inhaling the past
at future's expense

she's stopped now, she's
found her spot, where lies
lonely grass, overgrown
buttressing the storied
the faded stone

she kneels by the marker, digs
into her purse, pulls out

a scratch-and-win

three flat-shiny inches
that flash, brazen and unreal
in the afternoon sun

she puts nail to ticket, scattering
still-born papery ash, over old
sleeping earth

try again, it says
and she rises, disappointed

yet lighter, somehow

Emily Carr's grave, Ross Bay Cemetery, Victoria, BC

from the diary of a green poet

Sunday
woke from dream of carless world,
bicycles everywhere, the ring of their bells
music to match the reclaimed *fortissimo*
of birdsong

Monday
on the way to work, walked through
a new poem, the ravine full of Fall,
my colorized eyes suspended, leaf-style
for awhile

Tuesday
cancelled paper delivery, yesterday's news
screaming, of the death of trees,
my guilt a glossy flyer caught
between caffeinated headlines

Wednesday
electiontalk shrills the air, and I imagine
a grizzly perking its ears, listening, for its name,
hearing only the *brring* of machines
registering cash, registering cash

Thursday
bought more recycled envelopes for submissions;
I like to think this paper the resurrection
of paper used by writers past,
including 30% post-poet fibre

Friday
at a club, through clouds of multinational nicotine,
a bar band introduced a song as
Blues For Edward Abbey, and I think
maybe there's hope for the world

Saturday
woke from weird hangover dream of the last
Christmas tree, lit by the plume and pomp
of perched songbirds, the presents around its uncut trunk
the tears of a planet, watering the tree

pigeon at gatwick

> London calling, yeah, I was there too
> An' you know what they said?
> Well, some of it was true!
> — The Clash, "London Calling"

London called The Clash in '79, and now
London keeps calling me,
the city seeping through souvenir glue,
well-walleted tube tickets,
emptied knapsacks full of memories

in an irreverent reverie,
you imagine the Entombed of Westminster Abbey
leaving their stone and marble beds,
kings and queens and poets past
making their way to one of those all-over
fire-red phone booths, ancient eyes agog
at the phone sex cards stuck
to the booth's inner walls like a teen's
wallpaper dream, selecting, say,
"Young, Busty and Willing!"
and dialing;   musty, awakened fingers
alive with the thought
of this new country, its new flesh
only digits away

the past breathes down the present's
neck in this city, Dickens' *David Copperfield*
one shelf away from Nick Hornby's fidelities
and B-sides

you kick back in pubs
built in the Brontés' day,
unsoberly expecting the Sisters to

burst through the oak doors
sashay to the bar and down great jugs of ale,
their flushed, defiant eyes defying
their delicate, centuries-old reputations

in museums and galleries, you're glutted
with the Greats, the Real Things (almost)
too vivid, too brimming, for eyes born
of their pale-faced book-version imposters;
in the National Gallery, no glass
covers the canvases;
your artless fingers could touch Titian
touch Rembrandt, touch Van Gogh:
this thought   is enough

Soho, the Thames, Picadilly, Covent Garden—
sights enough for sore blink-believing eyes
pacing tube trains and blushing double-deckers

thankfully, you soon grow desensitized
to all this splendor,
concentrating on the important things,
like looking for the perfect
Big Ben T-shirt

inside Gatwick airport, baggaged and tagged,
trip almost over, you watch a pigeon
peck its way between rush-hour
runners and heels,
indoor suits and ties and purses oblivious
to the feathered kamikaze
at the mercy of their time-travelling
jet-lagged feet

miraculously, the bird
continues to dodge and duck
limb after limb after limb,
and you wonder what flight
the bird came in on,
and if it too wonders briefly
at where it might properly belong

eye surgery poker and the cat's whiskers

after the fifth time it's still my name
when finally wheeled into the OR,
and it's still the right eye that will glare
Cyclops-like up at the thousand-watt
lights, cloth covering your face save for
that right eye-hole cut to paste

it's time; a nurse tells you if you have to cough
to let them know, and you wish she hadn't said that
because now the idea of NOT coughing seems like life
or death, and how many coughs give you advance notice?

minutes later it becomes apparent that a bit more
anesthetic wouldn't have hurt, but stoicism prevails
and besides, you wouldn't want to interrupt the animated
chat between the surgeon and some nurses about
a recent staff poker game and how the men always win,
ha, ha

ha—how much longer will this last
you wonder, you wish you gave a damn about poker
because man it would be a godsend
if you could at least overhear an *interesting* conversation
as your cornea places its bets;
at some point the doctor mutters something about
"a technical challenge," and you pray an agnostic's
prayer that they're still talking about the game

hand me that, the doctor says and the nurse says
this? and you wonder what nameless implement
will next be making its mark on you and geez,
shouldn't they know its name?

you're holding your breath, determined not to
cough, and you conjure the image of your late cat—
your mind's eye sits him on your chest, his green
eyes pooling yours, his regal lynx lines realer
than this room, whiskers a millimeter away

nobody asks what this cat's doing in the OR
perched on this patient's chest, nobody
bats an eye, but he gets me through it
my cat does, the doctor's declaration of
a successful operation its cue to jump off
to go back and wait for me,
under the living green

later, gratefully munching some post-op
toast, I wonder at all the things that must
necessarily pass unseen before surgeon's eyes,
those other bits of worlds
brushed away with a tissue,
by their winning hands

you, sleeping

are you sleeping now, continents away
across this city's river, the night
the blanket we share, switch-on stars
the night's light keeping monsters
at bay

i like to think you're sleeping now,
your mind drained of all but
dreams that you navigate
with the twitch of divining limbs

i imagine you sleeping, buoyant
as you crest the shores of sheets,
your eyes never so open as when
they close, dark-to-dark

seeing maybe me, here, across
the river, my curled and sleeping form
a kind of question mark waiting
for an answer

just beginning

in less than a year JFK's brain-blood will redden
between the lines of every black and white

now's the time to make a move
so I make mine

it's a good night for it—

the day's arguments have been hampered
with the rest of the dirty laundry
the low-fi is serenading silence with Gould's fugues
the record-setting BPM (barks-per-minute) black lab
is outside nipping at stars, where he belongs

my future mom is in the mood.
"Volunteer Queen" has landed a shiny new Red Cross station wagon
to expedite her good works,
and today a co-worker playfully confused her with Anne Baxter

future dad has heard rumorings of a raise at work,
and tonight Bach talks wonders to him
through Glenn's wizard variations

the day's clothing is quickly doffed, it's history
and I hold my breath as a bed springs to life

soon it is that moment, and I swear the dog suddenly stops barking
as if sensing competitive yelps on the horizon

dad's timed it well, Bach and Gould climaxing their own coital act
and I leave dad for mom
whose hugging arms begin the welcome that will never outstay

dad collapses relieved, lighter now
my journey sealed with a slick kiss
and less than a year later JFK is shot, life over
mine just beginning

Acknowlegements

Alice Major and Jade O'Riley for their invaluable help early on;

Special 'DeNiros' to Linda Rogers, for keeping the faith;

Sub-group shout-outs to my 1996 P.O.P gang, and much gratitude to Sari Friedman-Rosner and Dr. Stephanie Mitchell, who saw some light in my darkest days;

My parents (you know who you are);

My brother Tim Schumm for his superb cover photograph;

Various muses (real and imagined);

Ruth Linka & Lee Shedden at Brindle & Glass;

the Alberta Foundation For The Arts;

and all those friends over the years who kept asking when The Book was coming!

— The title poem "What We're Left With" placed first in the *Contemporary Verse* 2000 poetry contest judged by Di Brandt.

— "Journey's End" won Honorable Mention in the 1998 *VUE Weekly* Modern/Traditional Poetry Contest.

— "Brand New World" was a finalist in *THIS Magazine*'s 2000 Great Canadian Literary Hunt.

— "The Licorice Man" placed third in the 2001 International Petra Kenney Poetry Awards, London, England.

— "Breaking the Surface" placed first in the 2001 Canadian Poetry Association Awards.

— "Head-Smashed-In Buffalo Jump" was a finalist for the 2002 Sandburg/Livesay Award.

— "Garage Sale" was a finalist for the 2002 *fiddlehead* Ralph Gustafson Poetry Prize.

— "Cat Standard Time" received an Honorable Mention in the 2004 Cranberry Tree Press anthology competition.

— "You, Sleeping" placed third in the 2005 *Contemporary Verse 2* Great Canadian Love Poem Contest.

The title of the poem and of section 3, "The Whole Earth an Inn for the Night," is a line from the Franz Kafka story "The Hunter Gracchus."